Are you ready for an Art Attack?

Send friends & family a special message with a unique Art Attack card! I have shown you how to make different types of cards, you can use the ideas to make up a few of your own!

So if you're ready to make some cards turn the page and let's have some Art Attacks!

Editor: Karen Brown   Designers: Ant Gardner/Darren Miles
Artist: Paul Gamble   Craft Maker: Susie Johns

THIS MAD COW MAKES A GREAT GREETINGS CARD - YOU COULD USE IT FOR SOMEONE'S BIRTHDAY OR JUST TO SAY HELLO!

You will need:
Thin card, scissors, felt tip pens, glue.

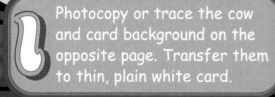

1 Photocopy or trace the cow and card background on the opposite page. Transfer them to thin, plain white card.

2 Colour the cow and the grassy background using felt tip pens or coloured pencils and then cut both pictures out.

3 Fold them both in half along the dotted lines.

4 Glue the cow's feet tabs to the four rectangles on the card background to complete.

WRITE YOUR MESSAGE INSIDE THE CARD AND SEND!

Happy Valentine's!

1 Photocopy or trace both parts and transfer them to thin, plain white card.

2 Colour in both sections and cut them out including the speech bubble.

3 Secure the parts together by pushing a paper fastener through the middle.

TURN THE DIAL TO WHAT YOU WANT TO SAY AND THEN SEND TO YOUR VALENTINE!

TELL THEM TO REPLY BY TURNING THE DIAL AND SENDING IT BACK!

BE MY VALENTINE ?

In your dreams!

Oh, yes please handsome!

I'm yours forever!

Love is blind... ...I'm not!!

Whatever!

You will need:

Thin card, scissors, felt tip pens, glue, paper fastener.

6

BON VOYAGE!

KNOW SOMEONE WHO'S GOING ON HOLIDAY OR ON A LONG TRIP - SAY BON VOYAGE!

YOU WILL NEED:

YOU WILL NEED:

Thin, white card, scissors, coloured pens or pencils.

1 Photocopy the background card and the rocket on to plain white paper.

2 Stick the pictures onto thin card and carefully cut them out. Make slits where marked with the dotted lines on the front of the card.

3 Colour both parts in using felt tip pens, making sure the pieces match.

4 Fold the background piece in half along the dotted lines and then thread the rocket piece through the slits.

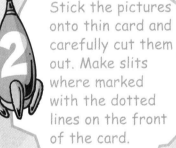

Funky Fairies!

good luck!

hello!

CREATE SOME CRAZY COLLAGE CARDS BY STICKING LOTS OF BITS 'N' PIECES ON TO COLOURED CARD.

You will need

Coloured card, glue, glitter, sequins, coloured paper.

1 Fold a piece of coloured card in half to form the background card.

2 In pencil, trace one or both of the fairy templates onto the front of card.

3 Cut out leg, arm and head shapes from skin coloured paper and stick these on the card with paper glue.

4 Cut out a dress and wing shapes and stick these in position. Add a crown on the head.

5 Decorate the outfits with glitter, sequins and fake jewels. You could create a wand from a star jewel if you have one.

6 Draw a face on your fairy and finally write a message inside the card.

USE THIS IDEA TO MAKE OTHER COLLAGE CARDS!

it's a girl!

Get Well

CHEER SOMEONE UP WITH A HAND-MADE GET WELL CARD!

1 Photocopy the card onto white paper.

2 Stick it onto thin card or thick paper and cut it out.

3 Fold the card along the horizontal dotted lines.

4 Now fold the card along the vertical dotted lines.

5 Colour the card in using coloured pencils or felt tip pens.

6 Finally write your message and deliver!

From your mate James!

YOU WILL NEED:

Thin, white card or thick paper, scissors, coloured pens or pencils.

From

11

SAIL AWAY!

SAY HAPPY BIRTHDAY WITH A STAINED GLASS EFFECT CARD!

YOU WILL NEED:
Coloured card, acetate or see-through packaging, 3D paints, sticky tape.

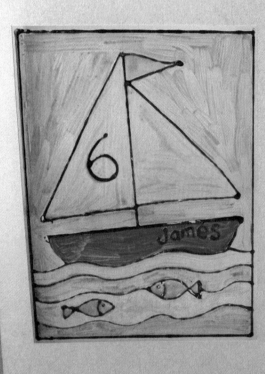

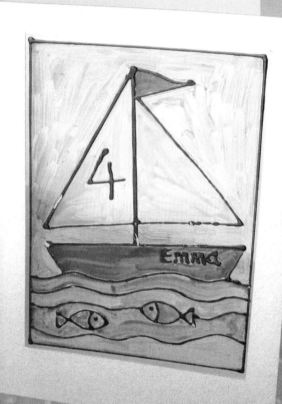

 1 Cut a piece of card to size and fold in half. Carefully cut a large rectangle out of the front.

 2 Trace the sailing boat on to the acetate or see through packaging using black 3D paint and leave it to dry.

3 Using the other 3D paints, colour in the the rest of the picture and leave to dry again. (You can add the person's age to the sail.)

 4 Now stick the picture to the background card from the inside, keeping it neat and tidy.

 5 Write your message and send!

PARTY INVITE!

MAKE YOUR OWN UNIQUE ART ATTACK PARTY INVITES! JUST FOLLOW THE STEPS BELOW..

YOU WILL NEED:

Thin card, scissors, glue, felt tip pens.

Alex's Birthday

21st June

6 - 8 pm

43 South Street

Fancy Dress!

R.S.V.P.

IF YOU WANT TO MAKE LOTS OF INVITES YOU WILL HAVE TO PHOTOCOPY THE CARD MANY TIMES.

1 Photocopy panel 1 and panel 2 once and photocopy panel 3 twice onto plain white paper.

2 Take a piece of thin card and stick panel 3, panel 2 and the second panel 3 next to each other on one side. Trim the card and then stick panel 1 on the reverse of the first panel 3.

3 Fold in both side pieces and then colour the whole thing in.

4 Carefully cut out the windows on the second panel 3.

5 Finally write your invite on the inside left-hand side and send.

14

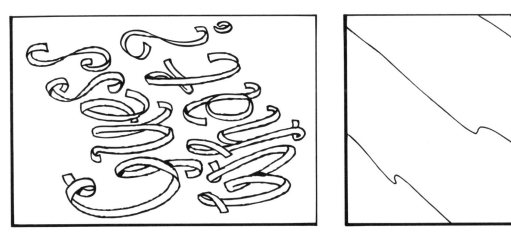

Easter Card

SAY HAPPY EASTER
WITH THIS COOL
CONCERTINA CARD!

You will need:

Thin card, scissors, glue,
colouring pens.

1 Photocopy the card onto plain white paper and stick it onto thin card.

2 Colour the whole thing in using felt tip pens and then fold along each of the dotted lines to form a concertina shape.

3 Finally write a message on the back and send.

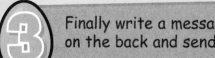

Birthday Card!

MAKE SOMEONE A STAR FOR THE DAY ON THEIR BIRTHDAY!

You will need:

Thin card, scissors, glue, colouring pens, photograph.

1 Photocopy the card onto plain white paper and stick it onto thin card.

2 Cut the whole card out and then carefully cut out the TV screen section and remove.

3 Colour everything in using felt tip pens and then fold the card in half along the vertical dotted lines.

4 Stick a photo of the birthday girl or boy on the inside so you can see it through the TV screen.

5 Finally write a message on the inside and send!

cut out
this
section

Happy
Birthday

ENVELOPE CARDS!

HOW ABOUT MAKING A CARD AND ENVELOPE IN ONE?
THESE CARDS ARE TO SEND YOUR CONGRATULATIONS BUT
YOU CAN MAKE THEM WITH AN ALTERNATIVE MESSAGE.

YOU WILL NEED:

THIN CARD,
SCISSORS,
FELT TIP PENS

WELL DONE

1 Photocopy the cards onto white paper and then stick them onto thin card.

2 Cut them both up and then colour them in on both sides.

3 Fold the sides of each card along the dotted lines, so that the flaps fold inwards.

4 Write a message inside and close with a sticker.

USE THE TEMPLATES TO MAKE YOUR OWN CARDS. TRACE THE SHAPE ONTO CARD AND THEN DRAW YOUR OWN PICTURE IN THE MIDDLE.

WELL DONE!

On The Move!

KNOW SOMEONE WHO IS MOVING HOUSE OR LEAVING TOWN? THEN THIS IS THE CARD FOR THEM!

You will need:

Thin card, scissors, felt tip pens, paper glue.

1 Photocopy the card pieces onto white paper and then stick them onto thin card with paper glue. Colour everything in.

2 Cut all the pieces out. Carefully make slits where with solid lines on the main picture at sections A, B and C.

3 Fold the card in half along the horizontal line and then fold each of the three sections A, B and C forward so they stick out.

4 Using paper glue, stick the tree on B, the house on A and the bushes on C. Let them dry before folding the card in half again.

5 Write your message anywhere you like and send.

MOVING PARTS!

CARDS WITH MOVING PARTS ARE VERY EFFECTIVE AND SIMPLE TO MAKE.
HAVE A LOOK AT THIS CHRISTMAS CARD, THEN TRY A FEW OF YOUR OWN!

YOU WILL NEED:

Thin card, scissors, felt tip pens, coloured card, 3 paper fasteners.

1 Photocopy the card and smaller pictures onto white paper and stick them onto coloured card.

2 Colour Santa Claus in using your felt tip pens making sure that the arms and legs match the main picture.

3 Cut the main card out. Carefully cut along the large dotted line above Santa's head and fold the card in half so he stands up.

4 Make a slit below Santa and make holes where marked at points a, b and c.

5 Make holes on the smaller pictures and then attach them to the main picture. Secure a to a, b to b and c to c with paper fasteners.

6 Finally write in the card and send!

MAKE OTHER MOVING PARTS CARDS.
GO ON, TRY IT YOURSELF!

24

PENGUIN POP-OUT!

1 Photocopy the picture onto white paper and stick it onto thin card. Cut it out.

2 Fold it in half along the vertical dotted line.

3 Carefully cut the small red dotted line and fold the other dotted lines to push the beak outwards.

4 Finally, write a message on the back!